THE
GREAT
WITCH
HUNT

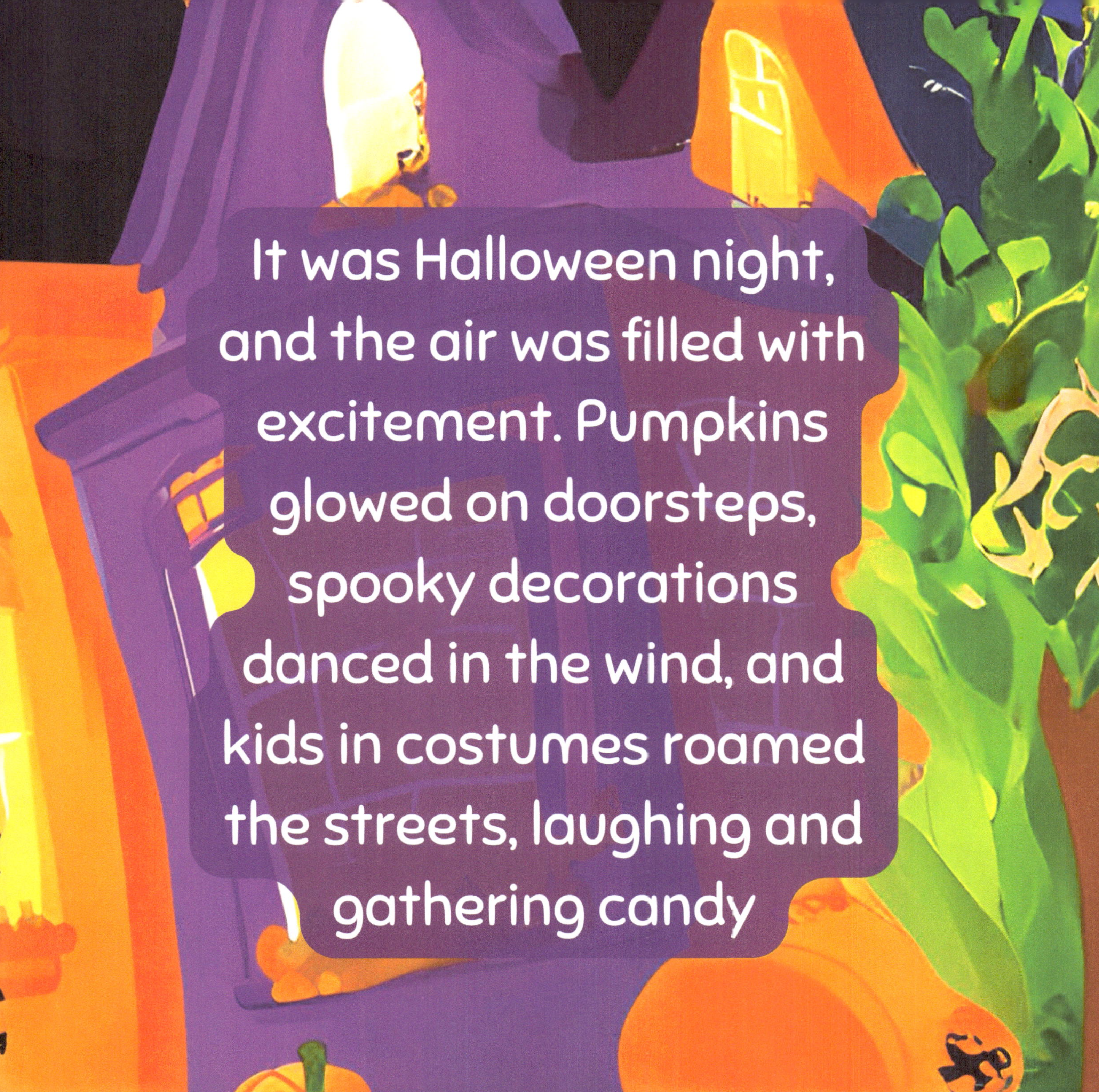

It was Halloween night,
and the air was filled with
excitement. Pumpkins
glowed on doorsteps,
spooky decorations
danced in the wind, and
kids in costumes roamed
the streets, laughing and
gathering candy

But something strange was happening—every time someone checked their candy bag, it was empty!

Two best friends, dressed up for trick-or-treating, were determined to figure out what was going on. "There must be a witch stealing our candy!" one of them said, eyes wide with determination. "Let's catch her!"

The two friends raced home, eager to come up with a plan.

They knew witches
loved magical
things, so they
decided to set a
clever trap.

First, they carved the biggest pumpkin they could find, covering it in sparkly glitter and hanging fake spider webs all around it.

"No witch will be able
to resist this!" they
said, placing the
pumpkin on the front
porch.

Inside the pumpkin, they hid a jar of sticky honey, hoping to catch the witch red-handed.

Next, they left a broomstick by the pumpkin—just in case the witch needed a quick escape.

Once everything was ready, they hid behind some bushes, their hearts pounding with excitement. The moon was full, casting a spooky glow over the neighborhood.

After a while, there was
a soft whoosh in the air,
and a shadow flew
across the sky.
"It's her!" whispered
one of the friends.

The figure swooped down on a broomstick and landed gracefully on the porch, her long cloak fluttering behind her.

The witch spotted the glittery pumpkin and couldn't resist taking a closer look. As she reached inside, her hand got stuck in the honey!

The two friends leapt
from their hiding spot.
"We've got you!"
they shouted.

But instead of being angry, the witch laughed—a warm, kind laugh that echoed in the night. "You clever children!" she said with a twinkle in her eye.

"I wasn't stealing your candy. I was protecting it from the greedy goblins that roam around on Halloween night!"

The friends blinked in surprise. "Goblins?"

The witch nodded. "Every Halloween, they try to take the best treats for themselves. I was just keeping your candy safe until the coast was clear."

Feeling a bit
embarrassed, the
friends apologized.
But the witch just
smiled.

"No harm done," she said. "In fact, let me give you a little extra for being such smart detectives."

With a wave of her hand, the witch filled their bags with the biggest, brightest candy they had ever seen

The kids looking amazed as their candy bags fill up with glowing, oversized treats.

"Happy Halloween!" she called as she hopped back on her broomstick, soaring into the sky with a trail of sparkling stars behind her.

The friends, with their candy bags full and smiles wide, waved goodbye. It had been the best Halloween adventure yet.

Boo! May your
Halloween be
filled with treats
and no tricks!